Helping Children See Jesus

ISBN: 978-1-64104-000-6

Faith
Old Testament Volume 2: Genesis Part 2

Author: Arlene Piepgrass
Illustrator: Vernon Henkel
Computer Graphic Artist: Andrew Cross
Typesetting and Layout: Morgan Melton, Patricia Pope

© 2018 Bible Visuals International
PO Box 153, Akron, PA 17501-0153
Phone: (717) 859-1131
www.biblevisuals.org

All rights reserved. No part of this publication may be reproduced, stored in a retrieval system or transmitted in any form by any means, electronic, mechanical, photocopy, recording or otherwise, without the prior permission of the publisher, except as provided by USA copyright law.

RELATED ITEMS

To access related items (such as activities, memory verse posters and translated texts) please visit our web store at shop.biblevisuals.org and enter 2002 in the search box on the page.

FREE TEXT DOWNLOAD

To access a FREE printable copy of the teaching text (PDF format) in English or other available languages, enter S2002DL in the search box. Add the item to your cart, and use coupon code XTACSV17 at checkout. Once your order is processed you will receive an email with a link to the free download.

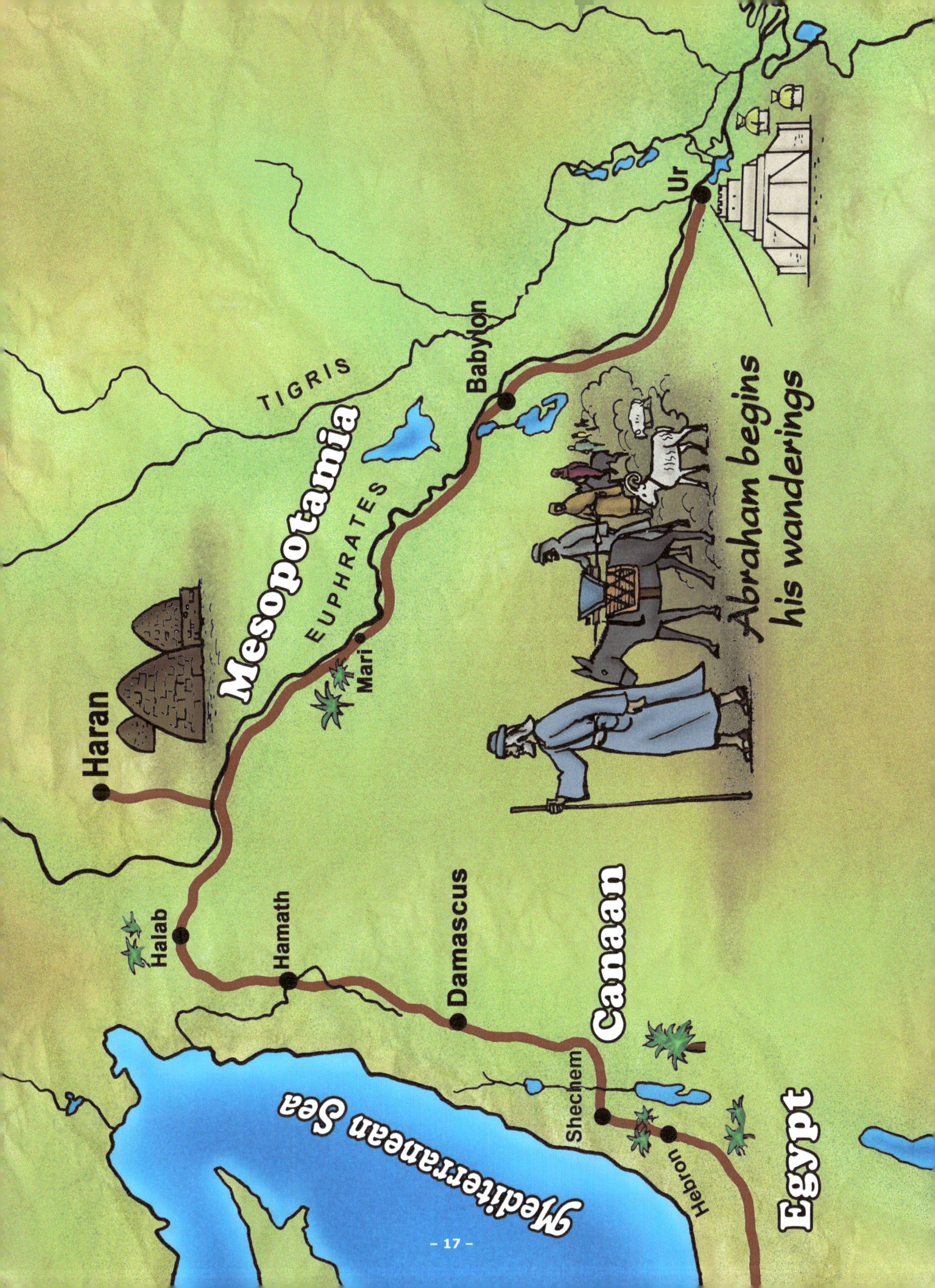

But without faith it is impossible to please Him; for he that cometh to God must believe that He is, and that He is a rewarder of them that diligently seek Him. Hebrews 11:6

Lesson 1
THE OBEDIENCE OF FAITH

Scripture to be studied: Genesis 11:31; 12:1-9; Acts 7:2-4; all verses in the lesson.

The *aim* of the lesson: To show that the result of true faith is obedience to the Lord.

What your students should *know*: That God commands and honors obedience.

What your students should *feel*: A desire to obey the Lord.

What your students should *do*: Seek to know God's will and do it.

Lesson outline (for the teacher's and students' notebooks):
1. The home of Abram.
2. The command of God (Genesis 12:1-3; Acts 7:2-3).
3. The response of Abram (Genesis 11:31; Acts 7:4).
4. The altar of worship (Genesis 12:4-9).

The verse to be memorized:

But without faith it is impossible to please Him; for he that cometh to God must believe that He is, and that He is a rewarder of them that diligently seek Him. (Hebrews 11:6)

NOTE TO THE TEACHER

The back cover has a map showing Ur, Haran, Canaan, Mediterranean Sea, Euphrates River and Chaldea.

The Word of God is the living seed that brings everlasting life. We are born again, nurtured and prepared for service by the power of the Word of God. Encourage your students to study the Word for themselves. Remember that "Faith cometh by hearing, and hearing by the word of God" (Romans 10:17).

THE LESSON

God created Adam. But sin spoiled Adam's life. Sin spoiled the lives of Adam's children and his grandchildren. People became so wicked that God had to destroy all living creatures except the few who obeyed Him: Noah and his family. God began again with Noah, but as the years passed people forgot God and went their own way again.

Instead of worshiping God, they began to worship the sun and moon which God had created. Using wood and stone, they carved images that looked like themselves. Then they set them up and worshiped them. They called the images "gods." How foolish! How sinful!

Could gods of wood and stone hear them when they prayed? Could such gods answer their prayers? Could the sun and moon help them when they cried for help? Never! Only the living God, whom they refused to worship, could hear and answer prayer.

As men forgot God, they began making plans to become powerful and famous. Those who were leaders called an important meeting to promote a new idea. (See Genesis 11:3-4.)

"We'll build a city with a tower that will reach to Heaven," the spokesman said. "The tower will be seen for miles around. We'll become famous. Everyone will admire us and fear us. In this way we can control all the people on earth."

"A tremendous idea!" they agreed. "When shall we begin?"

"Immediately," was the answer.

God had commanded them to scatter over the earth and populate it. (See Genesis 9:1.) Instead, they disobeyed God and began to build a tower that would unite them in one place.

As God looked down on all they were doing, He said, "Will men ever obey Me? Will they ever pray to Me and ask Me to show them what to do? I'll show them that I am the Lord God, the ruler of Heaven and earth. Now they all speak the same language. I'll cause them to speak different languages so they won't be able to understand each other." (See Genesis 11:5-9.)

The next day the foreman gave orders as the men gathered to work.

"What did you say?" the workmen asked. "We can't understand you. What language are you speaking?"

Those who laid bricks couldn't understand those who carried the bricks to them. Those who carried water to mix the mortar couldn't understand the ones who were mixing.

The leaders called another meeting. "How can we continue our project with so much confusion?" the spokesman asked.

But even those in the meeting couldn't understand each other. Finally they simply had to give up and stop building the city and the tower!

God showed His power once again and forced the people to scatter over the earth as He had planned.

Those who spoke the same language settled in areas together and continued their lives as usual. But alas, they failed to worship God. They failed to realize that He was the One who stopped the building of the tower.

1. THE HOME OF ABRAM

Some of these people settled in an area called Chaldea. There they built a big city on the banks of the Euphrates River and named it Ur. (*Teacher:* Point to these places on map–back cover.) Many people went to this city because in Ur they could make a good living for their families. Ships loaded with ivory, silver and copper sailed into Ur. For these luxuries the people of Ur traded their dates, corn, fruits and grain. So business prospered.

Because the river made the farmland fertile, many farmers and herdsmen went to live in Ur. Education was important to the people. They built a great library. They developed industry. They made pottery, musical instruments, gold and silver statues and jewelry.

The people of Ur were religious. In fact, their city was built around the highest hill of the land on which they erected a beautiful and expensive temple to the moon god. Priests and priestesses served in the temple, offering sacrifices to this false god. The people of the city and surrounding areas came regularly to the temple to worship. On special feast days the statue of the moon god was carried on the shoulders of men who paraded through the city. Later it was returned to its place on the top of the high temple.

A young boy named Abram lived with his father (Terah) and his brothers (Nahor and Haran) in Ur. Abram and his brothers helped their father care for his herds of animals. They went to school and learned to read and write. They watched the ships unload at the docks. They went to the big temple of the moon god with their father. (See Joshua 24:2.)

When Abram became a young man, he married a beautiful girl named Sarai. They had many friends in Ur, and life was happy and pleasant for them. Abram continued working with his father and became wealthy. He owned many animals himself. He had servants to help him and Sarah with the work.

But deep in his heart Abram had a longing which all his wealth and his comfortable home and many friends couldn't satisfy. God was making him dissatisfied with the idol worship all around him in Ur.

The Bible doesn't record the conversations Abram and his father had, but they could well have been something like this:

Show Illustration #1

"Father, do you believe that statue to the moon god in the temple can help us?" Abram asked. "Do you really think it is that god which gives us good harvests and pasture for our flocks? How could a god of gold do that? We know the man in Ur who molded the statue for the temple. There can be no power in that idol."

"But, Abram," replied his father, "everyone sacrifices to that god. Everyone worships at the temple. They'll criticize us if we stop going to the temple with them. They'll blame us if the rains do not fall. We can't stop offering sacrifices to the moon god."

"Father, I can no longer go to the temple with you. The idols have no power. They have no life. I refuse to worship them any longer. I truly believe there must be a living God who has created us and who is ruler over us," said Abram.

2. THE COMMAND OF GOD
Genesis 12:1-3; Acts 7:2-3

Show Illustration #2

The day came when the true and living God Himself spoke to Abram.

"Abram," God said, "I want you to leave this country and its people. I want you to leave your relatives. I will show you where to go. Pack your belongings. Gather your flocks and your servants. Prepare for a long journey.

"Abram, you will not be sorry if you obey Me. All the people of the earth are following their own way. They worship idols. They refuse to hear My voice. I am going to make a new nation and you will be the father of it. I will bless you, Abram. Whatever you do will be successful. I will make your name great. You will be a blessing to others. Through you all the nations of the earth will be blessed."

The command of God was perfectly clear. It wasn't hard for Abram to understand what God wanted him to do.

The promises of God were wonderful. But if Abram wanted to enjoy the promises, he had to do what God commanded. It wasn't enough for him to say, "Yes, God, I believe You can bless me as You promised. I believe You want me to leave Ur." He had to obey God, proving that his faith in the living God was real.

3. THE RESPONSE OF ABRAM
Genesis 11:31; Acts 7:4

As a good husband Abram shared the command of God with his wife. "Sarah," he said, "I don't know where God is going to lead us. I do know the trip will be hard for you. But God has promised to bless us if we obey Him completely. He has promised that if I leave my homeland and my father, He will give me another land and make me the father of a great nation. We know He is the living God. He can and will do what He has promised," Abram explained.

"But, Abram, how can God make you the father of a nation when we do not have children?" Sarah asked.

"I don't know," Abram replied simply. "I only know what God promised. And I believe He will do what He says."

Excitement ran through the household of Abram as orders were given to pack and prepare for a long journey.

"I wonder where we're going," a servant said as she carefully laid Sarah's clothes in a basket.

"No one seems to know," her helper answered.

"Which god told Abram to leave here?" asked the first.

"They say the living God has spoken to Abram. You know our master has refused to worship the idols in the temple. He will not allow any idols in his household. He says there is only one God, the living God who created everything and who rules over His creation."

Meanwhile Nahor, Abram's brother, tried to discourage him.

"Why do you want to leave? There's plenty of pasture here for our flocks. It will be dangerous to take such a journey with Sarah. There are robbers on the road. They might kill you so they can take Sarah for themselves. You ought to stay here."

"Nahor, I must obey God. He has spoken to me and commanded me to leave. I cannot stay. I know He will care for us."

"Well, where are you going?" Nahor wanted to know.

"That I can't answer. God hasn't yet told me where to go. I know only that I must start. I believe He will guide me each day," Abram replied firmly.

"Do as you wish. But I think you're foolish," Nahor insisted. "So does everyone else."

"God has spoken. God has promised. God will take care of us." Abram spoke confidently. But he may have wondered if Nahor was right. Yet by faith he continued his preparations to leave. (See Hebrews 11:8.)

Show Illustration #3

The day came when everything was ready for the long trip. It's never easy to say good-bye and there must have been many tears.

"Oh Sarah, we'll miss you! Will we ever see you again?" her relatives and friends asked.

"I don't know," replied Sarah with tears in her beautiful eyes. "I know only that my husband must obey God. And I am happy to go with him wherever God is leading us."

Mounting her camel, Sarah wrapped her shawl over her head to protect herself from the sun and dust. Waving farewell, she rode behind Abram and his father (Terah) as they led the large caravan of servants and flocks from Ur of Chaldea.

"I'm glad our nephew Lot has decided to go with us," Abram remarked. "He'll be a big help to us in caring for the herds and flocks." (Had Abram forgotten so quickly? God had told him to leave his land *and* his relatives. But his father and nephew went with him. See Genesis 11:31-32; Acts 7:2-4. Was he completely obedient?)

Each evening the travelers set up their tents, fed the animals, built fires to cook their food. Each morning they broke up camp and continued their journey.

Days, weeks and months went by. They became weary. Sarah would often ask, "Abram, are you certain God is leading you?"

"Yes, I know He is. He has promised to bless us. We're obeying His command. He will not disappoint us. Nor will He fail us," Abram said encouragingly. (See Hebrews 11:8.)

Abram loved and worshiped the true and living God of Heaven. But his old father did not. He worshiped false, make-believe gods. (See Joshua 24:2.) So when they had traveled about 600 miles, they came to the city of Haran. (Show map.) God had not told them to stop there. But Abram's father was not interested in the living God. So they all settled in Haran. Years later, the old father died. (See Genesis 11:32.) Now at last, Abram was separated from his father. And again God spoke to him. Again Abram packed up his possessions and he, Sarah and his nephew Lot moved on.

4. THE ALTAR OF WORSHIP
Genesis 12:4-9

Weeks, maybe months, later they arrived in the land of Canaan. There God appeared to Abram, saying, "Abram, *this* is the land I am going to give to your children!"

What a joyful day this was! If Abram had refused to obey God, he would have missed this. God assured him again that He had led and He was going to do what He had promised.

Abram built an altar with stones at this spot where God appeared to him. He killed some of his animals and offered them on the altar as a sacrifice to God.

Show Illustration #4

Abram, his wife (Sarah), his nephew (Lot) and his servants gathered around the altar (Genesis 12:7). There Abram worshiped God, saying, "My God, I thank You for leading us safely to this spot. I thank You for blessing us. I thank You that You will continue to guide us each day."

God never fails anyone who obeys Him. He commands us in Proverbs 3:5, 6 to trust Him and not to depend on our own wisdom. Often we don't know what to do. But God tells us that if we look to Him and listen to Him, He will direct our paths.

God declared Abram righteous (in right standing with God) because Abram believed Him (Romans 4:3). God will also declare us righteous if we believe that His Son, Jesus Christ, died on the cross for our sins and rose again (Romans 4:5).

God has a plan for the life of each one, just as He had for Abram. How will you respond? Will you say, "Here am I, Lord, use me!" Or will you say, "I want my own way; don't bother me, Lord!"

The Lord promises us, "I will never leave thee nor forsake thee" (Hebrews 13:5). As we obey Him, we can boldly say, "The Lord is my helper, and I will not fear what man shall do unto me" (Hebrews 13:6).

Someday the Lord might want you to be a pastor or missionary or a teacher. But right now the Lord wants you to be born into His family. He wants to forgive your sins. Right now the Lord wants you to obey Him. Right now He wants you to tell your friends that He died for them also. He wants you to be kind and loving to those around you.

God wants to direct your life just as He wanted to direct Abram's life. Will you let Him do that?

Lesson 2
THE WEAKNESS OF FAITH

Scripture to be studied: Genesis 12:10-20; 16:1–17:8, 15-27; 18:1-15; 20:10-12, 14; 21:1-8.

The *aim* of the lesson: To show that, even though we fail, God is always faithful.

What your students should *know*: That we do not need to fail.

What your students should *feel*: God can keep us trusting Him.

What your students should *do*: Depend on the Lord to keep us following Him today.

Lesson outline (for the teacher's and students' notebooks):
1. Failure to trust God for provision and safety (Genesis 12:10-20).
2. Failure to believe God's promise (Genesis 15:1-6; 16:1-16).
3. Failure to experience God's peace.
4. Faithfulness of God in spite of Abram's weakness (Genesis 17:1-8, 15-27; 18:1-15; 21:1-8).

The verse to be memorized:

But without faith it is impossible to please Him; for he that cometh to God must believe that He is, and that He is a rewarder of them that diligently seek Him. (Hebrews 11:6)

NOTE TO THE TEACHER

Teachers are not born; they are made. A good teacher must be willing to be taught himself/herself. The more you depend upon the Holy Spirit, the more usable you will be as you teach God's Word. Do you really believe God and take Him at His word? Only as you trust Him yourself can you encourage your students to put their complete confidence in Him.

THE LESSON

Abram and Sarah and the many servants who had come with them to the new land settled down to a daily routine of activity. They were now in the place to which God had led them. The shepherds took the flocks of sheep and goats and the herds of cattle to find pasture each day. The women were busy cooking meals and washing clothes.

1. FAILURE TO TRUST GOD FOR PROVISION AND SAFETY
Genesis 12:10-20

Day after day the sun shone brightly. Week after week went by with no rain. As the shepherds returned to the tents one evening, they spoke to Abram: "Master, every day it is harder to find grass for all the animals. We go farther and farther away but everything is dried up. If we don't soon have some rain, the animals will starve."

"Maybe it will rain tomorrow," replied Abram hopefully.

But the next day the sun shone brightly as usual, drying the ground and burning the bit of grass that remained.

"Our gardens are drying up. Where are we going to find food to eat?" asked Abram's servants.

Probably some of the servants became dissatisfied and began to grumble, "Why did we ever come here? We should've stayed back in Ur where we always had plenty to eat."

But who had brought Abram and his family and servants to this place? *(God)* Do you think God could now take care of them and provide what they needed? Yes, He's the One who sends the rain, and He is able to supply all of our needs. (See Philippians 4:19.)

Abram should have built an altar and thanked God for His care. He should have asked for wisdom to know what to do. Instead, Abram began making plans to move. What a mistake to leave the place to which God had led him! What a mistake to leave this land which God had promised to give him!

But giving orders to his servants, Abram commanded, "Prepare to take down the tents. Load everything we own on the animals. Herd the animals together. Prepare food for a trip. We're leaving Canaan and going south to Egypt. We'll die if we stay here. We can come back later when the rains have come."

How grieved God must have been! "Oh, Abram, I could take care of you and give you enough food if you would just stay where I've led you. Pray to Me before you move."

But Abram did what he thought was best. He was walking by sight, not faith.

Show Illustration #5

As they neared the border of Egypt, Abram became worried about his safety. Confiding to Sarah, he said, "My dear, you are a beautiful woman. When the men in Egypt see you, they will try to kill me so they can have you for a wife. Since you're also my half sister (Genesis 20:12), tell them you are my sister so they won't harm me."

How do you suppose God felt when He saw Abram planning and scheming to protect himself?

Abram forgot how God had protected him and Sarah all the way from Ur to Canaan. He forgot that God had promised to bless him and make him the father of a great nation. Instead of trusting God, he planned to lie.

Just as Abram had feared, the men in Egypt thought Sarah was beautiful. They told the king about her. Thinking she was Abram's sister, the king gave Abram animals and servants in exchange for Sarah.

"Oh, Abram, must I leave you to go to live with the king? Will I ever see you again?" Sarah sobbed.

"Don't worry, my dear. When the famine is over in Canaan, we'll return there together," Abram assured her, as Sarah was led away to the palace.

It didn't please God that Abram and Sarah had left Canaan. He was not pleased that they had lied. He could have said, "Abram, you can stay here in Egypt forever since you prefer this to Canaan which I chose for you. I shall bless someone else."

That is what Abram deserved. But God does not deal with us as we deserve (Psalm 103:10-11).

God still loved them. So in some unexplained way, God told the king that Sarah was really Abram's wife, not his sister.

Calling Abram to the palace, the king asked, "Why did you lie to me? Why did you tell me Sarah is your sister? Take her and leave our country at once!"

How thankful Abram and Sarah were to be together again! If only they had trusted God, they would never have been separated.

Sarah exclaimed, "Oh, it feels good to be going home to Canaan!"

"I am sorry, Sarah," Abram said, "that I didn't trust God. I'm sorry I made it so hard for you. As soon as we get back to Canaan, I am going to build an altar and thank God for protecting us and leading us back to the place He chose for us."

And that is exactly what Abram did. (See Genesis 13:4.)

2. FAILURE TO BELIEVE GOD'S PROMISE
Genesis 15:1-6; 16:1-16

We might suppose that Abram would never forget God's promise. Surely he would never again forget to ask God to guide him. But Abram was like we are. Again he forgot God's promises and began to make his own plans.

You remember when God called Abram to leave his home, He promised that Abram would be the father of a great nation. But ten years had gone by since they had come to Canaan. Abram and Sarah were getting old. Still they had no children.

Show Illustration #6

One night Abram was wondering how God would keep His promise. God called him outside and said, "Abram, look up into the sky and count the stars. How many are there?"

"Oh, God, I can't count all of them. There are too many," Abram replied.

God promised, "Abram, that is how many descendants (children, grandchildren, great grandchildren, etc.) you are going to have–more than you can count."

"I don't understand how this is possible," Abram responded. "But I believe what You say, my God. I believe You will do what You've promised."

"Because you believe Me, Abram, you are in right standing with Me." That is what God meant when He told Abram he was righteous because he believed God. (See Genesis 15:6.)

But as time went on, Sarah became impatient. She doubted that God would really give her a baby. One day she came to Abram with an idea. Following the custom of Ur, she said, "We have waited and waited for God to give us a baby, Abram. I do not believe He is going to do so. So you take my servant, Hagar. Maybe God will give us a son with her."

But Abram and Sarah were different. They had followed the living God. God didn't want them to do what the people of Ur did. He wanted them to trust Him.

Again Abram forgot to build an altar and pray to God before making such an important decision. He listened to Sarah's suggestion instead. "Maybe you're right, Sarah," he said. "Maybe God wants us to have a son through the help of Hagar."

But if that's what God had wanted Abram to do, He would have told him! Again Abram made plans without asking God for direction. Months later a little boy named Ishmael was born to Hagar in Abram's home. But this was not the baby God had promised to give Abram and Sarah.

3. FAILURE TO EXPERIENCE GOD'S PEACE

Show Illustration #7

Quickly Abram learned that disobedience to God brings sorrow instead of joy. Sarah was sad as she watched little Ishmael. This wasn't her baby. She became jealous of Hagar, Ishmael's mother, and treated her unkindly.

Hagar was unhappy because Sarah was sharp and impatient with her. Abram was sad because of all this. No one was happy.

God wasn't pleased either with Abram's actions. God had promised him a son through Sarah. God hadn't told Abram *when* He would give him that son. But God always keeps His promises. He wanted Abram to trust Him and patiently wait for Him, instead of making his own plans. The impatience of Abram and Sarah brought only heartache.

4. FAITHFULNESS OF GOD IN SPITE OF ABRAM'S WEAKNESS
Genesis 17:1-8, 15-27; 18:1-15; 21:1-8

Thirteen years went by and Abram didn't hear God's voice. But God still loved Abram and Sarah. He knew that they really wanted to obey Him, even though they sometimes made wrong decisions because they forgot to ask Him what to do.

When Abram was 99 years old and Sarah was 89, God again spoke to Abram.

"Abram, I am going to change your name. From now on you will be called *Abraham*, or *father of many nations*. I am going to make you, Abraham, a father of many nations. Also I am going to give you and Sarah a baby boy next year at this time."

"Oh, God, you can't possibly do that. I will be 100 years old. Sarah will be 90. Old people can't have a baby!"

"That's right, Abraham," God answered. "Old people like you can't have a baby. But *I* am going to give you a son. I can do the impossible because *I AM* Almighty God. Nothing is too hard for Me!"

What a wonderful promise! The living God of Heaven can do the impossible!

Show Illustration #8

Just as God promised, one year later little Isaac was born to Abraham and Sarah. Twenty-five years had gone by since God had first promised a son to Abraham. (See Genesis 12:2-4.) Abraham and Sarah were not always faithful to God during those years, but God was faithful to them. What joy and happiness rang out in their home as they watched Isaac grow! Oh, how they thanked God for keeping His promise! They praised God that He had forgiven their disobedience. How grateful they were for God's love which never changed! Abraham and Sarah were so changeable–sometimes doing the will of God, sometimes doing what they wanted.

God who loved Abraham and Sarah loves us. He wants to direct our lives. God wants to bless us. Often we act like Abraham and Sarah. We don't pray to God when we must make decisions. We don't read His Word. We don't believe His promises. We become impatient when we don't get immediate answers to our prayers. We make our own plans so that we get the answers we want.

But God keeps on loving us. He is patient with us. (See Psalm 103:8, 10, 11.) He keeps on forgiving our disobedience when we ask Him to forgive us (1 John 1:9). He not only forgives our sins, He forgets them.

God has promised us eternal life if we believe that Jesus Christ is His Son who died on the cross for our sins. (See John 3:16; 1 John 2:15.) God will keep this promise. (See Titus 1:2.)

God also has promised that those who will not believe that His Son died on the cross for their sins will be punished in the lake of fire forever (John 3:36; Romans 6:23; Revelation 20:13-15). God will likewise keep this promise. Which promise do you want fulfilled for you?

Lesson 3
THE TESTING OF FAITH

Scripture to be studied: Genesis 13; 18; 19; 22.

The *aim* of the lesson: To show that God tests our faith in Him to make us trust Him more and depend on Him completely.

What your students should *know*: Testing comes from God for a purpose.

What your students should *feel*: Confidence that God tests us to strengthen us.

What your students should *do*: Trust God today even though we don't understand all our circumstances.

Lesson outline (for the teacher's and students' notebooks):
1. Testing Abraham's desires (Genesis 13).
2. Testing Abraham's concern (Genesis 18:1-33; 19:1-26).
3. Testing Abraham's love (Genesis 22:1-14).
4. Testing is a part of God's purpose (1 Corinthians 10:13).

The verse to be memorized:

But without faith it is impossible to please Him; for he that cometh to God must believe that He is, and that He is a rewarder of them that diligently seek Him. (Hebrews 11:6)

NOTE TO THE TEACHER

Are you familiar with the spiritual needs of your students? Determine how you are going to minister to these needs and prepare your lessons accordingly. Be sure to spend time in prayer as you study your lessons, that the Lord will suit them to the experiences of your class.

THE LESSON

When everything is going well for us, we often forget God. We forget to thank Him; we forget to pray to Him. We sometimes forget that we need Him. God sends problems and difficulties into our lives to teach us to depend on Him. He wants us to become strong Christians who will bring glory and praise to Him. He knows that when He tests us, we will become stronger if we look to Him for help. (See James 1:2-4.)

God brought many trials into the life of Abraham. He wanted to make him a useful man of God. These trials are recorded in God's Word so we can learn what to do when difficulties come into our lives. (See 1 Corinthians 10:11.)

1. TESTING ABRAHAM'S DESIRES
Genesis 13

When Abraham and Lot returned from Egypt, they were both wealthy men. (See Genesis 13:2, 5.) Each possessed many servants, tents, gold and herds of animals.

Sadly, the herdsmen of Lot and those of Abraham began to argue and fight for the best pasture for their animals.

"We were here first," Lot's herdsmen said. "You find another place for your flocks."

"But our master is greater than yours. *You* find another place. We should have the best pasture for Abraham's flocks," Abraham's servants answered. "Get out of the way so we can water Abraham's flocks!"

"Wait your turn! Our animals are drinking now."

So day after day they quarreled.

Show Illustration #9

When Abraham heard about it, he called Lot to him.

"Lot, this fighting between our herdsmen must stop. You're my nephew. I love you. I don't want any misunderstanding between us. Besides, we serve the living God. Fighting doesn't honor God. Our neighbors here in Canaan know we believe in the God of Heaven. If they see our servants arguing and fighting, they'll think the true God is no better than the gods they serve.

"Look at all the land around us, Lot," continued Abraham. "There is plenty for both of us. You choose where you want to live. I will take what you do not choose."

Abraham was older. He was the leader of the family. Lot should have let him choose first. But Lot wanted an easy life. He thought only of himself, and he wanted the best. Looking around as far as he could see, he thought, *Since I have first choice, I'll pick the best land. There's plenty of water down there along the Jordan River. The pasture looks richer and greener. There are two big cities there, too—Sodom and Gomorrah. I think that area would be an easy and comfortable place to live.*

"Uncle Abraham, I think I'll go east. My family and servants and I will settle near the city. Thank you for letting me choose. I hope things will go well with you." And Lot moved his entire household to the place he had chosen. He didn't ask God to show him where he should go. He made the choice himself.

Seeing Lot move away, did Abraham feel lonely? Did he feel that he had second best? The Bible doesn't tell us. But if he did, he soon felt differently because the Lord spoke to him.

"Abraham, look as far as you can see to the north, south, east and west. I'm giving to you and your descendants all the land you can see. I'm going to give you so many descendants you won't be able to count them. Abraham, I want you to enjoy the land. Walk through it, look it over. It's yours!" promised Almighty God.

Abraham built an altar and worshiped God.

"I thank You, dear Lord, for choosing for me. Your choice is the best. I believe You will give me all You have promised." Abraham truly wanted whatever God chose for him.

2. TESTING ABRAHAM'S CONCERN
Genesis 18:1-33; 19:1-26

Many years went by, and Lot had moved right into the city of Sodom. Abraham continued to live in a tent in the place God had chosen for him. One day three strangers stopped at Abraham's tent with a message. These were not ordinary visitors. Two were angels. The third was the Lord Himself!

"Abraham," the Lord said, "you have obeyed Me. You've led your household to obey Me. Because you are blessed of God, I will tell you what I'm going to do" (Genesis 18:17-21). God honored Abraham's faith and obedience and confided in him as a friend.

"The cities of Sodom and Gomorrah have become so wicked that I am going to destroy them," the Lord continued.

Abraham could have thought, *Now selfish Lot will get what he deserves.* Instead, fear struck Abraham. *Lot and his family live in Sodom*, he thought. *If God destroys the city, they too will be killed!*

Show Illustration #10

Abraham responded, "Oh, Lord, if you find 50 godly people in Sodom, You will not destroy them with the wicked, will You?"

"No, Abraham, if I find 50 godly people there, I will not destroy Sodom. I'll save the whole city for their sakes," answered the Lord.

"Oh, my Lord," prayed Abraham again, "if you find just 45 godly people, will you destroy the city?"

"No, Abraham, I will even save it for 45 godly people," the Lord promised.

Abraham continued pleading with the Lord to spare Sodom: "If there be 40, 30, 20, 10!" And the Lord promised He would not destroy the city, even if He found only ten godly people.

Abraham was concerned for Lot and his family. He knew the Lord would answer prayer. This is why he prayed for them.

But there were not even ten godly people in the cities of Sodom and Gomorrah. However, God heard Abraham's prayers. He knew Abraham's heart. He knew how much Abraham cared for his nephew, Lot. And so the angels took Lot, his wife, and his two daughters out of Sodom before God caused fire to fall, destroying the city. (See Genesis 19:15, 24, 25.)

"Do not look back at the city! Run for your lives!" the angels commanded. "If you look back, you will die!" (See Genesis 19:17.)

But Lot's wife loved the city so much that she couldn't resist looking back. Immediately she turned into a statue of salt. She was dead just as the angels had warned! (See Genesis 19:26.)

Lot had chosen what looked like the best place, the easy place, the comfortable place. Now he lost everything he owned, except two daughters. How much better it would have been if Lot had asked God to show him what he should choose and where he should live.

Abraham let God choose for him. He worshiped God. Abraham had power with God through prayer. He believed God and God answered his prayers. If Abraham had not prayed, Lot too may have been killed. God will hear your prayers for your family, your friends. (See John 14:13, 14.)

3. TESTING ABRAHAM'S LOVE
Genesis 22:1-14

God had another test for Abraham that was harder than all the others. You remember in our last lesson we learned that Abraham and Sarah waited 25 years for little Isaac. How happy he made their home! As they watched him grow, they knew it was through Isaac that God would give them many descendants as He had promised.

One night God gave Abraham a strange order. "Abraham, I want you to take your son, Isaac, whom you love dearly. Go to the land of Moriah. There I'll show you a mountain on which I want you to build an altar to me. I want you to offer Isaac as a sacrifice.

My only son! thought Abraham. *How will I have numberless descendants as God promised if Isaac dies? But God makes no mistakes. I do not understand why He has asked me to offer Isaac but I will do what He says. If need be, I know He can bring Isaac back to life to keep His promise.* (See Hebrews 11:17-19.)

No, Abraham didn't know why God gave him this strange command. He didn't know what God was going to do. But *God* knew what He was going to do. He wanted Abraham to believe Him and obey Him.

Abraham could have said, "My God, show me how You are going to give me many grandchildren and great grandchildren if I offer up Isaac. Then I'll do it. Show me first. Then I'll obey You."

Instead, early in the morning Abraham prepared for the journey. It wasn't easy to obey such a command. But he didn't delay. He took the wood he would need for the sacrifice and loaded it on his donkey. Two servants went along. Isaac was accustomed to his father's offering sacrifices to the living God. He didn't know that this time *he* was to be the sacrifice.

The third morning of their journey, as Abraham looked at the mountains ahead of him, God said, "Abraham, that is where you are to offer Isaac."

To his servants, Abraham said, "You stay here while Isaac and I go on to worship the Lord. We will be back." Abraham believed they would both return. He didn't understand how, but he trusted God.

Taking the wood off the donkey, he put it on Isaac's shoulders. As they walked, Isaac turned to Abraham. "Father," he said, "I see you have a knife and a flint to start the fire. I have the wood. But where is the lamb we are going to sacrifice to God?"

"My son, God will provide the offering for us," said Abraham confidently.

Maybe there will be a lamb on the mountain top when we get there, Abraham must have thought. *If not, how will I tell my beloved Isaac that he must be the sacrifice?*

On the mountain they built the altar. Then Abraham explained what God had commanded.

Show Illustration #11

Isaac loved and trusted his father. He willingly obeyed him. He let his father tie him. Without struggling, he lay on the altar.

Abraham took the knife and raised it to slay Isaac. At that moment the Lord called, "Abraham! Abraham!"

"Here I am, Lord," answered Abraham.

"Do not touch Isaac. You have shown Me that you truly love Me. You were willing to give Me that which is dearest to you– your only son."

As Abraham looked around he saw a ram caught in a bush nearby. Just as he had said to Isaac, God did provide the animal for sacrifice. And Abraham quickly put the ram on the altar in Isaac's place. What praise and thanksgiving Abraham felt in his heart to Almighty God!

"Abraham, I have seen that you will not keep back anything from Me," said the Lord. "I will bless you richly. Through you, I will bless all the nations of the earth because you have obeyed Me. Your descendants will be more numerous than the stars in the sky or the sand on the seashore."

4. TESTING IS A PART OF GOD'S PURPOSE
1 Corinthians 10:13

God wanted Abraham to know who He is and what He is like. This is why God tested Abraham. Each test caused Abraham to know God better and to trust Him more.

First, God commanded Abraham to leave his home country and go to the land where God would lead him. Abraham believed and learned that God kept His word.

Later, God caused Lot and Abraham to separate. By letting God choose for him, he learned that God's choice was best.

Six times God promised to give Abraham a son. But God made Abraham wait more than 25 years to receive the promised son. Abraham learned that God keeps His promises in His time.

The final test was the hardest. God had prepared Abraham to obey Him even though what He commanded was hard to do and impossible to understand. Without questioning God, Abraham obeyed. When God spoke and rescued Isaac, Abraham trusted God more than ever. He knew he would never need to be afraid to obey any of God's commands.

God tests each one who belongs to Him but He has promised not to test us more than we can stand. (See 1 Corinthians 10: Because God knows everything and we know nothing, we should obey Him without question. He is good and His plans are best for us. Because He is wise and loving, we should obey His commands for He knows what is best for us. When we obey, God blesses us more than we ever expect.

Show Illustration #12

God commanded Abraham to offer his only son, Isaac. Abraham obeyed and, at the last moment, God provided a substitute sacrifice.

Years later, God did not spare His only Son. (See Romans 8:32.) The Lord Jesus went all the way. He died on the cross of Calvary, the perfect sacrifice for our sins. God loved His Son, the Lord Jesus Christ, far more than Abraham loved Isaac. Yes, God loved us enough to send His Son to die for us. However, He loves His Son so much that He won't accept anyone into Heaven who refuses to believe that Jesus died for his/her sins. Do you believe this? Are you depending on Jesus Christ *alone* to get you to Heaven? There is no other way. (See John 14:6.)

Lesson 4
FAITH REWARDED

Scripture to be studied: Genesis 15; Romans 3, 4; all verses in the lesson.

The *aim* of the lesson: To show the reward both now and eternally of believing God and obeying Him.

What your students should *know*: That the Christian life is the only worthwhile life.

What your students should *feel*: A desire to live as God commands in His Word.

What your students should *do*: Determine to obey the commands of God.

Lesson outline (for the teacher's and students' notebooks):
1. The gift of God: Justification (Romans 4:19-25; Genesis 15:6).
2. The reward of faith: Fellowship with God (1 John 1:3; 5:14-15; James 2:23; Mark 9:41; 1 Thessalonians 4:16-17).
3. Blessings from God for the faithful (John 14:27; Romans 8:35-39).
4. The believer's testimony before others (Genesis 23).

The verse to be memorized:

But without faith it is impossible to please Him; for he that cometh to God must believe that He is, and that he is a rewarder of them that diligently seek Him. (Hebrews 11:6)

NOTE TO THE TEACHER
Help each student to know he/she is accountable to the Lord for the way he/she lives and that God has something for each Christian to do. Nothing is more rewarding than discovering and carrying out the plan of God for our lives. Encourage your students to live for the Lord and serve Him.

THE LESSON
What is the difference between a gift and a reward? (Encourage discussion.) Can you earn (or merit) a gift? *(No)* How can you qualify for a reward? *(You do something to earn it.)*

In this final lesson on the subject of faith, we will discuss the most important gift of all and the rewards which follow it.

1. THE GIFT OF GOD: JUSTIFICATION
Romans 4:19-25; Genesis 15:6

When God called Abraham, commanding him to leave Ur, it wasn't because Abraham was better than others who lived in Ur. God didn't promise to give Abraham a son and make him (Abraham) the father of a large nation because he was a good man. Abraham was a sinner like everyone else. But Abraham believed God would do what He promised. So he left his home and followed the leading of God. (See Romans 4:3.)

Abraham didn't know when or how God was going to give him a son. He *did* know that he and Sarah were too old to have a son. But God made a promise. And Abraham believed God could do the impossible. (See Romans 4:19-22.)

It was as if God said to Abraham, "Because in your heart you believe Me, I will accept you into My family. You were born a sinner like everyone else. (See Romans 3:23.) But I forgive your sins. You trusted Me to give you a son even though you didn't understand how this could happen.

Show Illustration #13
"Abraham, because of your complete faith in Me, I am giving you eternal life. When you die, you will come to Heaven to live with Me."

This is what God meant when He said that because Abraham believed Him, he was justified or declared righteous. (See Genesis 15:6.) God counted Abraham as being in right standing with Himself. Why? Because Abraham believed God.

We are all unrighteous (sinful) when we are born. (See Romans 3:10, 12.) How can we be justified (declared in right standing with God)? How can we be accepted into the family of God and receive eternal life? We could never have forgiveness of sins by being good, because we couldn't be good enough. (See Isaiah 64:6.)

Eternal life is a marvelous *gift*. It cannot be earned. (See Romans 6:23b.) We must *believe* in our hearts that what God says is true. He says the Lord Jesus Christ is His Son. (See Matthew 3:17; 17:5; compare 1 John 4:14-15.) We must believe that the Lord Jesus died for us and receive Him as Saviour. (See 1 Corinthians 15:3-4; John 1:12.) When we place all our trust in the Lord Jesus, God gives us eternal life. He declares we are in right standing with Him through His Son, Jesus Christ. (See Romans 4:24-25; Isaiah 61:10.) God wants to give you His free gift of salvation. And you will receive it when you place all your trust in His Son. Is *your* faith in the Lord Jesus Christ?

2. THE REWARD OF FAITH: FELLOWSHIP WITH GOD
1 John 1:3; 5:14-15; James 2:23; Mark 9:41; 1 Thessalonians 4:16-17

After we're saved, God gives rewards to those who continue (diligently) to follow Him by faith. (See the memory verse: Hebrews 11:6.) The Christian life is a constant life of faith—looking to God for guidance, for provision, for everything.

Show Illustration #14
God wants us to enjoy friendship (fellowship) with Him. We may do this in at least four ways:

A. Through the Word of God
Abraham did not have a Bible because the Bible was not yet written. But God Himself often spoke to Abraham, giving him commands or promises. What a privilege to hear the voice of Almighty God! This was one of the rewards God gave to Abraham because of his faith and obedience.

As Abraham obeyed one command, God gave him another. When Abraham was disobedient, he sometimes did not hear God's voice for a long time. (*Teacher:* There is no reference of God's appearance while Abraham was in Egypt; nor between the birth of Ishmael and the renewed promise of Isaac.)

Later, the Word of God was written on scrolls. (Do you see the scroll in the illustration?) Today we have His Word in a Book—the Bible. And through His Word God speaks to us. He gives us His commands. He makes promises to us. He gives us His Holy Spirit in our hearts to teach us and help us understand His Word. What a privilege to read the Bible and hear God speaking to us! Did you read your Bible today? Did you ask God to speak to you today? Are *you* claiming this reward from God?

B. Through prayer

When Abraham heard the voice of God, he built an altar thanking Him for His leading and help. He thanked God for keeping His promises.

You and I can pray to God through the name of the Lord Jesus Christ. Think of it! God wants us to talk to Him. (*Teacher:* Point to the praying man in illustration.) This is one of the rewards of being in His family. We can actually talk with the Creator of the universe! (See 1 John 1:3.) We don't need to pray to someone or something else and ask that person or thing to pray to God for us. God tells us that we are to "come boldly to the throne of grace [the very throne of God], that we may obtain mercy, and find grace to help in time of need" (Hebrews 4:16).

Abraham had power with God through prayer. Because of Abraham's prayers, Lot and his two daughters were saved out of Sodom before God destroyed it with fire.

We, too, have power with God when we pray in the name of His Son, Jesus Christ. (See John 14:13-14; 1 John 5:14-15.)

C. Through hospitality

Three heavenly visitors came to Abraham's tent one day, Abraham said to them, "Come and rest awhile. Let me get water and wash your feet. Please stay and eat with me." (See Genesis 18:1-22.)

They were happy to accept his hospitality because Abraham was a friend of God. (See James 2:23.) The Lord commands us to show hospitality to others. (See 1 Peter 4:9; compare Hebrews 13:2.) He promises us a reward if we do it in His name. (See Mark 9:41.) When we entertain those who love the Lord and serve Him, it is as though we are entertaining Him. This is another reward God gives to those who have faith in Him.

D. Through prophecy

(Do you see the prophet preaching?)

God told Abraham His secrets because He knew Abraham loved and trusted Him. When the fire and brimstone from Heaven destroyed Sodom and Gomorrah, it was no surprise to Abraham. Why? Because God had told him He was going to do this.

Through His prophets God has told us that one day He is going to destroy this world. But He has promised that those whose faith is in Him will not be destroyed. They will be taken out of the world by the Lord Jesus before it is destroyed, just as Lot was taken out of Sodom before the Lord destroyed it. The Holy Spirit helps God's people to understand this. (See 1 Thessalonians 4:16-17.)

3. BLESSINGS FROM GOD FOR THE FAITHFUL
John 14:27; 15:11; Romans 8:35-39

God caused Abraham to become very rich. He owned many flocks and herds. He had many servants. He possessed gold. But these were not the things that Abraham counted important.

Abraham was looking toward his home in Heaven. (See Hebrews 11:10.) Abraham knew that all he owned could not help him enter Heaven. He knew he couldn't take his possessions with him when he died. He was interested in being blessed by God with things that would never perish.

God fulfilled every promise He gave to Abraham. Abraham became the father of a great nation which we know today as the Jewish nation–Israel.

Through this nation He gave us His Word–the Bible. (See Romans 3:2.) God reveals Himself to us through the Bible. All the nations of the earth are blessed as they read His Word.

Show Illustration #15

God chose a young Jewish woman named Mary to be the mother of His Son, the Lord Jesus Christ. Mary was a descendant of Abraham. (See Matthew 1:16-17.) So God fulfilled His promise to Abraham saying, "In your seed shall all the nations of the earth be blessed" (Genesis 12:3; 18:18; 22:18). All over the world, those who trust in Christ as Saviour are blessed by this Descendant of Abraham.

God does not bless everyone with wealth. But He does promise to bless everyone who is born again into His family with:

Peace of heart and mind (John 14:27)
Joy (John 15:11)
His love (Romans 8:35-39)

God wants us to look toward the heavenly city He is preparing for us. (See Colossians 3:1-2.) He wants us to be interested in His blessings which will never pass away.

> **NOTE TO THE TEACHER**
>
> To explain the meaning of *descendant* which appears in this paragraph, point to the many people pictured in the illustration. Mention that between Abraham and Mary there were many, many people: Isaac, Jacob, Kings David and Solomon–do you see the king in the illustration?–and a host of other *descendants*.

4. THE BELIEVER'S TESTIMONY BEFORE OTHERS
Genesis 23

All who knew Abraham watched him. They heard him talk about the one living God whom he worshiped. They saw by the way he lived that the God of Heaven was powerful and answered his prayers.

Show Illustration #16

A king came to Abraham on business one day, saying to him, "God is with you in all you do" (Genesis 21:22).

When Sarah died, Abraham went to his neighbors with a request: "My wife has died. I don't own any land in this country. I wish to buy a place to bury her. Will you sell me a piece of land?" (See Genesis 23:1-4.)

"Abraham, you're a mighty prince among us," they replied. "You may choose any place you'd like to have for a burying place for Sarah."

What a good testimony Abraham had before those who didn't know God! God rewarded Abraham because he had faith in God and believed Him. God gave Abraham the ability to live the kind of life which was honoring to Him.

What do your neighbors and friends say about you? God gives His children the Holy Spirit to live within them. The Holy Spirit gives believers the ability to live in such a way that others will know they love the Lord. The way a Christian acts is equally as important as the way he talks. Are you living as a Christian should?

Show Illustration #14

Are you reading the Word of God every day? Do you take time to talk with God each day? Are you being kind to others–doing nice things for them? Are you entertaining others in your home? Are you learning the secrets God has revealed about the future through His prophets?

List in your notebook those things you must do to be the kind of Christian God will reward. Then let's pray that God will help you do those things–beginning today.

www.ingramcontent.com/pod-product-compliance
Lightning Source LLC
Chambersburg PA
CBHW060801090426
42736CB00002B/114